SCHOLASTIC

Our Country
Write & Read Books

BY CATHERINE M. TAMBLYN

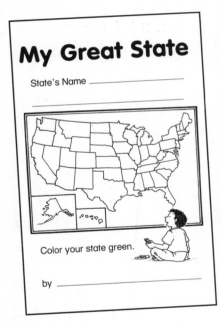

My Great State

State's Name _____

Color your state green.

by _____

The American Flag

by _____

I Celebrate Presidents' Day!

by _____

New York • Toronto • London • Auckland • Sydney
Mexico City • New Delhi • Hong Kong • Buenos Aires

D1372900

To HSM—Forever remembered and loved by me.
Smiles and peace, daddy.

Scholastic Inc. grants teachers permission to photocopy the reproducible
pages from this book for classroom use. No other part of this publication
may be reproduced in whole or in part, or stored in a retrieval system,
or transmitted in any form or by any means, electronic, mechanical,
photocopying, recording, or otherwise, without written permission of the
publisher. For information regarding permission, write to Scholastic Inc.,
557 Broadway, New York, NY 10012.

Cover design by Lillian Kohli

Cover illustrations by Maxie Chambliss

Interior illustrations by Maxie Chambliss, George Ulrich,
Anne Kennedy, and Ruth Linstromberg

Interior design by Ellen Matlach for Boultinghouse & Boultinghouse, Inc.

ISBN-13: 978-0-439-58849-2

ISBN-10: 0-439-58849-9

Copyright © 2006 by Catherine M. Tamblyn

Published by Scholastic Inc.

Printed in the U.S.A.

1 2 3 4 5 6 7 8 9 10   40   14 13 12 11 10 09 08 07 06

Contents

Our Country
Write & Read Books

Symbols & Holidays

People & Places

Introduction

Our Country Write & Read Books are an engaging way to build reading and writing skills while learning about social studies topics such as American symbols, holidays, geography, government, and more. Each book features predictable text that children complete. Some books invite children to draw illustrations. When finished, children will have their own personalized books that they'll be motivated to read again and again.

Since these books correlate to common social studies themes, they are easy to integrate into the curriculum. On pages 7–16, you'll find suggestions for introducing the books and making them, as well as ideas for extending learning. The books are also easy enough for children to assemble. Assembly directions appear on page 5.

Children will be proud to share their one-of-a-kind books at home and in school. Rereading the books and sharing them with others reinforces the concepts covered. Providing children with opportunities to read aloud also helps them develop fluency. Children will enjoy sharing their books as much as they enjoyed creating them, and they'll build skills and content knowledge in the process. Enjoy!

Connections to the Standards

These books are designed to support you in meeting the following reading, writing, and history standards outlined by Mid-continent Research for Education and Learning (McREL), an organization that collects and synthesizes national and state standards.

Reading
- Uses the general skills and strategies of the reading process.
- Uses reading skills and strategies to understand and interpret a variety of informational texts.

Writing
- Uses the general skills and strategies of the writing process.
- Uses grammatical and mechanical conventions in written compositions.
- Uses the stylistic and rhetorical aspects of writing.

History
- Understands the history of a local community and how communities in North America varied long ago.
- Understands the people, events, problems, and ideas that were significant in creating the history of their state.
- Understands how democratic values came to be, and how they have been exemplified by people, events, and symbols.
- Understands major discoveries in science and technology, some of their social and economic effects, and the major scientists and inventors responsible for them.

Source: *Content Knowledge: A Compendium of Standards and Benchmarks for K–12 Education* (4th ed.). Mid-continent Research for Education and Learning, 2006.

Getting Started With Write & Read Books

These books are designed for flexible use. Below are suggested guidelines for using the books in the classroom. Feel free to adapt any ideas to better meet the needs of your students.

Introducing the Books

Prior to having children create their books, it is helpful to introduce the social studies concepts to children, build background knowledge on the topics, and preteach any vocabulary words they will encounter in the text. It is a good idea to create a sample book in advance and read it aloud to children, pointing out the text and illustrations that you added to the book. This process will help children feel more confident when they create their own books.

Making the Books

The amount of guidance required as children work on their books will depend on their individual needs. If children need more support, create the books as a small-group or whole-class activity, having children complete a few pages at a time. You might work together to brainstorm possible responses for each page and record these on chart paper. Children can refer to the chart as they are writing. If students need additional support, you might have them dictate the text and then write it in dotted-line letters for them to trace.

Sharing the Books

Once children have finished their books, encourage them to read their books to themselves and provide opportunities for them to share their work with others. You might have children share their books with partners, with small groups, or with the whole class. To give everyone a chance to share, ask children to choose a page from their book to read to the whole class. Invite students to discuss their illustrations as well. Encourage students to ask questions and provide positive feedback about one another's work. Be sure to send the books home for children to share with their families. A letter is provided on page 6 to introduce Write & Read Books to families. A reproducible "About the Author" template appears on page 94.

Assembling the Books

Provide children with copies of the reproducible book pages and demonstrate the steps below. Or you might assemble the books in advance.

1. Carefully remove the perforated pages from the book. Make single-sided copies on standard 8½-inch by 11-inch paper.

2. Fold the front cover/back cover in half along the dotted line, keeping the fold to the left side.

3. Fold each interior page in half, keeping the fold to the right side.

4. Place the interior pages inside the cover and staple three times along the spine.

_____

Date

Dear Family,

Our class is making books that cover social studies topics and help children build reading and writing skills. These books include predictable text that is easy to read. They cover key topics such as geography, holidays, and government.

Each student adds writing and illustrations to complete the books and personalize them. The children are proud of their work and are eager to share it with you. We hope that you'll enjoy reading these books together. When reading the books, I encourage you to ask questions about the text or illustrations and provide positive feedback about your child's ideas, illustrations, handwriting, or overall presentation. You might also comment on your child's reading expression and fluency.

Thank you very much for your participation. Your encouragement will mean a great deal to your child.

Sincerely,

_____

Teaching Ideas

The American Flag

pages 17–20

The American Flag

by _____

Purpose

Children learn the features of the United States flag.

Strategies for Starting

Ask children to name colors they associate with the United States and to support their choices. Ask children to find an object in your classroom with the colors red, white, and blue. (*American flag*) Tell children that they will use the colors red, white, and blue in a book they will make about our flag.

Introduce the Book

Prepare a book as a model in advance. As you read the book aloud to children, point to the colors, stars, and stripes on your classroom flag. Recite the Pledge of Allegiance and invite children to demonstrate how they position their right hand over their heart when they say the pledge. Share that by reciting the pledge, Americans show that they honor our flag and our country. Point out that the United States flag stands for our country and its people.

Make the Book

Distribute copies of the reproducible book pages and assist children as they assemble their own books. As an alternative, provide children with preassembled books. Suggest to children that they refer to the classroom flag to help them color the illustrations.

Share the Book

Invite children to share their books with partners or in small groups. Suggest that they compare and contrast their responses on page 6. Encourage them to respond to their classmates' work with thoughtful questions and positive comments.

Beyond the Book

- Share the story of Betsy Ross with children. Examine the changes in the American flag over time.
- Relate the 13 stripes on the flag to a map of the 13 colonies. Count the 50 states on a United States map to correlate with the 50 stars on the flag.
- Provide background information about Flag Day. It marks the day in 1777 when the Second Continental Congress adopted an official flag for our new country. The first celebration took place June 14, 1877. It became an official holiday in 1949.

Symbols of the U.S.A.

pages 21–24

Symbols of the U.S.A.

by _____

Purpose

Children learn several symbols of the United States.

Strategies for Starting

Display a map of the United States and have children trace its boundaries. Define the word *symbol* for children, providing examples. Tell children that they will be making a book about symbols that stand for the United States. Explain that when people see these symbols, they think about our country. Provide children with brief background information on each symbol included in the book.

Introduce the Book

In advance, prepare a book as a model. Explain to children that U.S.A. is an abbreviation for United States of America. Show children photographs of the symbols featured in the book. Ask them if they recognize any of the pictures and where they may have seen these images.

Make the Book

Distribute copies of the reproducible book pages and assist children as they assemble their own books. As an alternative, provide children with preassembled books. Explain that on the last page, children will write about their favorite symbol for the United States.

Share the Book

Have children share their completed books in pairs, taking turns reading each page. Suggest that they compare their answers and discuss any differences. Invite children to share their symbol on page 6 with the class.

Beyond the Book

• Share the symbolism of the seven points in the Statue of Liberty's crown. (Each point represents a continent.)

• On a map, point out the locations of the Statue of Liberty (New York Harbor) and the Liberty Bell (Philadelphia, Pennsylvania).

• Study the bald eagle and its habitat.

• Search for items on which the symbols appear: U.S. postal mailboxes, stamps, and trucks; paper money; clothing; sports equipment; books; courthouses; vehicles; and so on.

We Honor Dr. King

pages 25–28

Purpose

Children learn about Dr. Martin Luther King, Jr., and the national holiday that commemorates his life.

Strategies for Starting

Provide children with background information about the time period in which Dr. Martin Luther King, Jr., lived. Then explain how Dr. King worked to make changes. You might read aloud a picture book about Dr. King. Explain to children that the title "doctor" does not always mean a medical doctor.

Introduce the Book

In advance, prepare a book as a model. Point out Dr. Martin Luther King, Jr., on the cover. Read aloud the book to children. Pause on each page to discuss possible responses.

Make the Book

Distribute copies of the reproducible book pages and assist children as they assemble their own books. As an alternative, provide children with preassembled books. Explain that on the last page, children will write about a way they can follow Dr. King's dream for peace.

Share the Book

Invite six volunteers to take turns each reading one page of the book to the class. Encourage them to discuss their responses. Invite everyone in the class to share the last page of their books. Compare and contrast their ideas and drawings. Children may enjoy sharing their own traditions observing Martin Luther King, Jr., Day.

Beyond the Book

• Create a bulletin board display titled "We Keep the Dream," using the last page of children's completed books.

• Share information regarding the struggle for equal rights. Discuss segregation in public schools, on public transportation, and in the use of restrooms and drinking fountains, as well as voting rights.

• Share background information about the Nobel Peace Prize. It was awarded to Dr. King in 1964.

I Celebrate Presidents' Day!

pages 29–34

Purpose

Children learn about George Washington, Abraham Lincoln, and Presidents' Day.

Strategies for Starting

Discuss what a leader is. Ask students to identify leaders in school groups, after-school programs, and so on. Explain that the president is the leader of our country. Tell children that they will be making a book about a holiday that honors past presidents.

Introduce the Book

In advance, prepare a book as a model. Use this book after students have studied George Washington and Abraham Lincoln. Before introducing the book, provide background information about the Revolutionary War and Civil War. Share picture books with students about Washington and Lincoln. Explain why Washington is known as the "father of his country" and Lincoln was called "Honest Abe." Read aloud the book to children. Pause and discuss possible responses for pages 6 and 7. Locate places mentioned in the book on a map (England; Virginia; Kentucky; Washington, D.C.).

Make the Book

Distribute copies of the reproducible book pages and assist children as they assemble their own books. As an alternative, provide children with preassembled books. For page 9, have children examine coins to look for Washington and Lincoln.

Share the Book

Invite children to share their books with partners or small groups. Encourage them to share their responses to pages 6 and 7 and to discuss any other information they know about Washington and Lincoln.

Beyond the Book

- Make paper stovepipe hats and tricornered Colonial hats to wear during a celebration of Presidents' Day.
- Set aside a special time for reading to celebrate Lincoln's love for books.
- Create a display with fun facts about Washington and Lincoln. Have children write or dictate facts they learned about these two presidents. Facts might include that Washington was the only president to have a state named after him and that Lincoln was the tallest president (6 feet, 4 inches). He was also the first president to wear a beard.

Happy Birthday, America!

pages 35–39

Purpose

Children learn about the history and traditions of independence.

Strategies for Starting

Lead a discussion about birthday celebrations and traditions, such as cakes, candles, and singing. Have children share their birth dates and ages. Tell children that they will be making a book about a birthday for something that is more than 200 years old. Challenge children to guess whose birthday it is.

Introduce the Book

Provide background information on the Revolutionary War. Share that the Fourth of July is another name for Independence Day. Read your prepared book to the class. Pause to discuss possible responses for pages that describe Independence Day traditions and celebrations.

Make the Book

Distribute copies of the reproducible book pages and assist children as they assemble their own books. As an alternative, provide children with preassembled books. Explain to children that on pages 4–8 they should draw pictures to match the text. On page 8 children can write about their own traditions for the holiday. Encourage them to think of something that was not included in the book.

Share the Book
Invite volunteers to read their books and share their pictures with classmates. Compare and contrast the variety of ways children celebrate Independence Day. Invite volunteers to share their own traditions celebrating this holiday.

Beyond the Book
• Create banners or posters about freedom.
• Share background information about Independence Day. It honors the day the American colonies adopted the Declaration of Independence. It was first celebrated on July 4, 1777, in Philadelphia. On that day, warships fired cannons, bells rang, games were played, and fireworks lit up the sky.

....
TEACHING TIP: At the end the school year, celebrate summer birthdays and Independence Day. Include this book as part of your celebration.
....

We Are Voters
pages 40–44

We Are Voters

by

Purpose
Children learn about Election Day and different ways to vote.

Strategies for Starting
Set up a situation in which your class will be divided in its opinion. Possibilities may include a choice of movies, books, and activities. Pose the choice in a question, such as "Which movie should we see? Which book should we read?" Ask children how they can make a decision as a class. Lead children to the conclusion that voting is a fair way to decide.

Introduce the Book
In advance, create a sample book as a model. Fill in page 2 with the choice posed at left. Read your book aloud to children. Provide children with background information about voting and our government. Discuss things children might see in their community that would alert them about an upcoming election, such as mailings and signs or voting booths in schools. Examine sample ballots.

Make the Book
Distribute copies of the reproducible book pages and assist children as they assemble their own books. As an alternative, provide children with preassembled books. Tell children to use the illustrations as clues to help them fill in the missing text.

Share the Book
Have children share their books with a partner or in a small group. Ask children if they have ever seen a voting booth, and invite them to share their experiences.

Beyond the Book
• Examine the Susan B. Anthony dollar and tell children that this famous American worked for equal rights for women, especially women's right to vote. Share a children's book about Susan B. Anthony.
• Identify the mayor of the children's community, the governor of their state, and the president of their country. Use a map to explain these different roles.
• Design a ballot box for classroom voting. Have children chart the results after voting.

....
TEACHING TIP: Make this book part of your study of citizenship, voting, or Election Day.
....

We Give Thanks

pages 45–49

Purpose
Children learn about the history of the first Thanksgiving. Children write about what they are thankful for.

Strategies for Starting
Ask children to recall situations in which they thank others and to tell ways they offer thanks—for example, verbally, by writing a note, or by giving a gift. Tell children that they will be making a book about a holiday on which Americans give thanks.

Introduce the Book
Provide background information on the Pilgrims, Wampanoag, and the first Thanksgiving. In advance, prepare a book as a model. Read aloud the book to children. Point out the picture you drew to show something or someone you are thankful for.

Make the Book
Distribute copies of the reproducible book pages and assist children as they assemble their own books. As an alternative, provide children with preassembled books. Tell children they will write about something they are grateful for on page 8. Encourage them to choose something or someone that is very important to them.

Share the Book
Have children share their books with a partner or a small group. Invite children to share page 8 of their books with the class.

Beyond the Book
- Have children write about other things they are thankful for. Invite them to illustrate their writing.
- On a map, trace the route of the *Mayflower*. Have children research life on the *Mayflower* and in Plymouth, Massachusetts.

- Compare the first Thanksgiving with Thanksgiving traditions today. Invite children to fill in a Venn diagram with this information.

The First Americans

pages 50–55

Purpose
Children learn about the food and shelter of four Native American peoples.

Strategies for Starting
Lead a discussion about the basic needs for food, clothing, and shelter and how people meet these needs. Discuss different types of homes, clothing, and foods, including examples from around the world. Tell children that they will be making a book about the first people who lived in America and how they met some of their basic needs.

Introduce the Book
Explain to children that a few hundred years ago in America there were no roads, stores, cars, planes, and so on. Provide background information on several Native American peoples (including those featured in the book) and discuss aspects of their cultures. In advance, prepare a book as a model. Read aloud the book to children. Pause while reading to discuss each group. Point out their general locations on a map (Iroquois—eastern New York to Ohio and Ontario to northern Pennsylvania; Sioux—the Great Plains of the Midwest; Hopi—northeastern Arizona; Makah—Washington State), and discuss the differences between these environments. Explain to students that there are many other Native American peoples.

Sensitivity Note: The text in this book uses the past tense in some places because it describes how these Native American peoples lived hundreds of years ago. Please impress upon your students that Native peoples still live in the United States today, participating in contemporary culture while still preserving their Native traditions.

Make the Book

Distribute copies of the reproducible book pages and assist children as they assemble their own books. As an alternative, provide children with preassembled books. Guide children to complete page 3 with the word *name*. Explain that there are several choices of responses for pages 4 and 5. For example, animals provided furs, hides, and food. Other parts of animals were used for different purposes as well. Provide references that show Native Americans in your state. Work with children to complete page 10.

Share the Book

Read the completed books as a class. Pause on pages 4 and 5 to allow children to share their different responses. Encourage children to share their final page with classmates.

Beyond the Book

- Create a bulletin board display using the last page of children's books.
- Study other Native American peoples from different regions of the country. Learn about how they met their needs for shelter, food, and clothing in addition to other aspects of their cultures.
- Show students a map that shows where different Native American peoples lived. Discuss the groups in each region.

Thank You, Inventors!

Thank You, Inventors!

pages 56–60

Purpose

Children learn about several inventors and their inventions.

Strategies for Starting

Introduce the term *inventor* as a person who thinks of an idea for something and is the first to make it. Explain that an invention is what is made. Provide small groups with a number of unrelated items, such as buttons, string, tape, straws, clay, pom-poms, spools, and waxed paper. Invite

children to invent something with the items and then share their inventions with classmates. Tell children that they will be making a book about inventors who invented some of the things they use today.

Introduce the Book

In advance, prepare a book as a model. Read aloud the book to children. As you read, pause to allow children to respond with the missing word (page 1: *day*; page 2: *phone*; page 3: *bright*; page 4: *fly*; page 5: *color*; page 6: *go*; page 7: *lunch*). Point out that most inventions from the past led to the creation of the newer models that are used today. Share background information about each of the inventors featured in the book.

Make the Book

Distribute copies of the reproducible book pages and assist children as they assemble their own books. As an alternative, provide children with preassembled books. Have children use clues in the illustrations to fill in the missing words in the text. On page 8, children draw and write about something they would like to invent. Encourage them to use their imagination.

Share the Book

Have children take turns reading the pages with a partner. Invite each child to share their invention on page 8 with the class.

Beyond the Book

- Research other inventions and their inventors. Create a bulletin board with text, drawings, and photographs.
- Create a bulletin board displaying page 8 of children's books.
- Have children create 3-D models of the invention they drew on page 8.

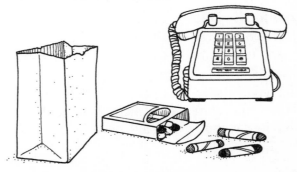

My Great State

pages 61–66

Purpose
Children learn about various aspects of their state, such as its capital, symbols, and places of interest.

Strategies for Starting
Display a map of the United States and have students locate your state. On chart paper, record a list of things that are special about the state, such as its climate, location, famous people, sports teams, products, attractions, landforms, bodies of water, and historical events. This book works well in conjunction with a study of your state. Provide books, brochures, maps, and other resources that children can use as reference as they complete their books.

Introduce the Book
In advance, prepare a book as a model. Read aloud the book to children. Begin by locating your state on the cover. As you are reading, pause to discuss each page. Ask children why they think the flower, tree, bird, and animal were selected to represent your state. Provide information about the special place and historical event you included in your book. Explain to children that they will choose different places and events in their books.

Make the Book
Distribute copies of the reproducible book pages and assist children as they assemble their own books. As an alternative, provide children with preassembled books. Work as a class to complete this book. Provide pictures and easy-to-read state books for reference as well as a list of special places and historical events that children may use as reference. Provide background information on these places and events. On page 1, have children complete the postcard by drawing a picture of a place in their state. Have them write the state's name on the line. On page 8, children can draw either the outline of their state or an illustration that shows something about their state's nickname.

Share the Book
Have children read their books with a partner. Then invite children to share with the class their responses on pages 2, 3, 9, and 10. Create a learning center about your state, with books, posters, postcards, maps, and other resources. Add the completed books to the center.

Beyond the Book
- Make an oversized picture map of your state, featuring wildlife, landmarks, products, and so on.
- Research the origin of your state's name.
- As a math link, find out how many years your state has been a state. Also count the number of counties it has.
- Examine the symbols on your state's seal and discuss why they were included.
- Create an alphabet frieze about places, people, and features of your state.

My Travel Book

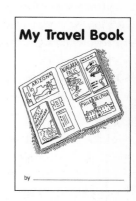

pages 67–72

Purpose
Children learn about several places of interest throughout the United States.

Strategies for Starting
Solicit from children the names of special places or things in the community, state, or country. List these places on chart paper. Ask them what is interesting about these places and why visitors might go to see them. Tell children that they will be making a book about some special places in different regions of the United States.

Introduce the Book
Explain what scrapbooks are and why people make them. If possible, show an example. Tell children that some people create scrapbooks about the

places they have visited. Explain that children will create a book that is like a scrapbook. In advance, prepare a book as a model. Read aloud the book to children. Display a map of the United States and use it to locate the states and places identified in the book. Explain that El Morro (also known as Inscription Rock) is part of El Morro National Monument and that Cliff Palace is part of Mesa Verde National Park.

Make the Book

Distribute copies of the reproducible book pages and assist children as they assemble their own books. As an alternative, provide children with preassembled books. Children will write state names in the blanks. They can use the map on each page for help with spelling. Have younger students write abbreviations instead. On page 10, children choose another place of interest. They might use the list of places on chart paper for ideas (see Strategies for Starting).

Share the Book

Have volunteers take turns reading each page of the book. Invite children to share with a partner any experiences they have had visiting special places. Encourage children to ask questions and share information about the places they have visited or about the places featured in the book.

Beyond the Book

- Make a bulletin board display, using page 10 of students' books.
- Locate and label the places featured in the book on a United States map.
- Study the places featured in the book. Show photographs of each place. Create a book of fun facts about these and other famous places.

Washington, D.C., Our Capital

pages 73–78

Purpose

Children learn about some of the buildings, monuments, memorials, and museums in Washington, D.C.

Strategies for Starting

Tell students that every country in the world has a capital city. Explain the importance of capital cities. Tell students that the capital city of the United States is Washington, D.C. Explain that it is neither a state nor part of a state. Explain that *D.C.* stands for District of Columbia.

Introduce the Book

In advance, prepare a book as a model. Read aloud the book to children. Explain that monuments and memorials are buildings, structures, or statues that honor a person or an important event. Also share that museums are buildings where people go to see interesting things, such as art, science exhibits, and history exhibits. Provide background information on the places featured in the book and show students photographs of them.

Make the Book

Distribute copies of the reproducible book pages and assist children as they assemble their own books. As an alternative, provide children with preassembled books. On each page, children fill in the missing text. They can use the labels on the illustrations as reference for spelling. On page 10, children write about another place in the capital, such as a monument, museum, or building.

Share the Book

Provide opportunities for children to read their completed books to classmates. Encourage them to share information about Washington, D.C., that they may know from visiting the capital or reading about it.

Beyond the Book

- Compare the spelling and discuss the meaning of *capital* and *capitol*.
- Identify monuments or memorials in children's own community. Describe and discuss what they honor or commemorate.
- Share background about Washington, D.C., and its history.
- Have students research and create a banner about places in Washington, D.C.

United States Geography Riddles

pages 79–84

Purpose

Children answer riddles and learn fun facts about the geography of the United States.

Strategies for Starting

Display a map of the United States or provide children with individual maps. To promote active map reading, ask questions, such as "Which two states are shaped like a rectangle?" (*Wyoming, Colorado*) "Which state looks like a pan?" (*Oklahoma*) "Which state looks like a boot?" (*Louisiana*) "Which state is the longest?" (*California*) Draw a compass rose with cardinal and intermediate directions (northeast, northwest, southeast, southwest), and ask questions regarding the location of states. Tell children that they will use a map to help them complete a riddle book about states, bodies of water, and other places in the United States.

Introduce the Book

In advance, prepare a book as a model. Read aloud the book to children. Allow children to guess the answer to each riddle. Have them look at a map of the United States to determine the answers. As an alternative, you might read the first two pages of the book to children to give them an idea of the book without revealing all the answers.

Make the Book

Distribute copies of the reproducible book pages and assist children as they assemble their own books. As an alternative, provide children with preassembled books. Allow children to work in small groups. Provide each group with a map of the United States to help them find the answers.

Share the Book

Have children read their books with partners, alternating pages. Invite children to share their riddles on page 10 with the class without naming the place. Have children guess the answers to the riddles.

Beyond the Book

- Use directions to describe the location of the places or things in the book.
- Write additional geography riddles about places in your town, community, or state. Or write additional riddles about different places around the country.
- Research and learn about each of the places featured in the book. Create a bulletin board with information about the places.

Our Government

pages 85–88

Purpose

Children learn about the three branches of government as well as laws, rights, and voting.

Strategies for Starting

Ask children who is in charge of your school. Explain that the principal is the leader of the school and that there are other leaders as well (teachers, vice principal, and so on). Ask children why these school leaders are needed. Then discuss why a country needs a government. Explain that each country has its own government. Tell students they will make a book about the government of the United States.

Introduce the Book

Label a diagram on chart paper with the president, Congress, and Supreme Court. Provide background information on these three branches of government. In advance, prepare a book as a model. Read aloud the book to children. Pause to discuss possible responses on pages 2 and 3.

Make the Book

Distribute copies of the reproducible book pages and assist children as they assemble their own books. As an alternative, provide children with preassembled books. On pages 2 and 3, students draw a picture and write about laws and rights. Recall some of the ideas discussed when you read aloud these pages to the class.

Share the Book

Invite children to read aloud their books with a partner. Encourage classmates to ask questions and provide positive feedback. Invite children to share with the class their responses on pages 2 and 3.

Beyond the Book

- Discuss why laws and rights are important. Create a list of classroom rules and rights. Phrase the rules in positive terms, such as "Put away materials" and "Walk quietly down the halls."
- Research and learn more about each branch of government. Make three large posters with information about each.
- Have students read about the current president or past presidents and share the information with the class.

Welcome to the White House!

pages 89–93

Purpose

Children learn about different places in the White House.

Strategies for Starting

Show children a photograph of the White House and ask them if they know who lives and works there. Provide background information about the presidency and the White House, including some historical facts and fun facts. Tell students they will create a book about the White House.

Introduce the Book

In advance, prepare a book as a model. Read aloud the book to children. If possible, show students photographs of each of the places mentioned in the book. Pause on each page to let children fill in the missing text.

Make the Book

Distribute copies of the reproducible book pages and assist children as they assemble their own books. As an alternative, provide children with preassembled books. Explain that children should use the illustrations as clues to help them fill in the missing text.

Share the Book

Invite children to share their books with a partner or small group. Encourage students to compare and discuss their responses.

Beyond the Book

- Have students add pages to the book that describe other places in the White House.
- Research fun facts about the White House. Create a bulletin board with the information.
- Create a time line of the presidents. Include photos and paintings to illustrate it.

The American Flag

by _____

Our Country Write & Read Books Scholastic Teaching Resources

What else do you know about our flag?
Draw a picture and write about it.

_____

_____

_____

7

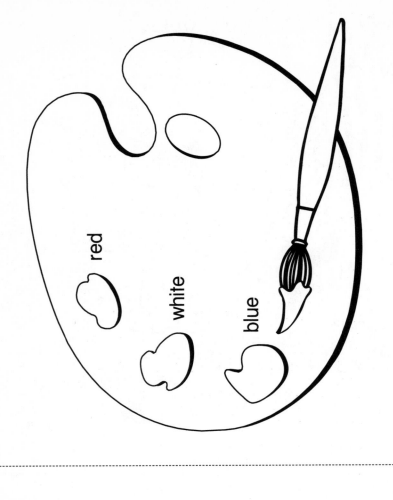

red

white

blue

See the colors of our flag.
The colors are red, white,

and _____ .

2

See our _____ flying high.
It is the flag of our country,
the United States of America.

1

Our Country Write & Read Books Scholastic Teaching Resources

See the stripes on our flag.

It has _____ stripes in all.

The stripes are red

and _____.

4

See the stars on our flag.

It has 50 _____.

Each star stands for a state.

3

Our Country Write & Read Books Scholastic Teaching Resources

We celebrate Flag Day

on _____.

On Flag Day, I like to

_____

6

We say the Pledge of Allegiance
to our flag.
I face the flag and put my

_____ over my heart.

5

Symbols of the U.S.A.

by _____

Our Country Write & Read Books Scholastic Teaching Resources

What else do you know about symbols of the United States? Draw a picture and write about it.

_____

_____

_____

_____

21

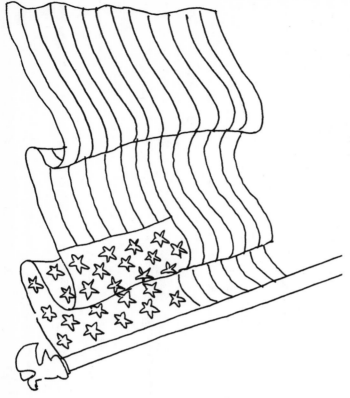

Many symbols make me think
of the U.S.A.
One symbol is the
American _____.
I see this symbol
_____.

2

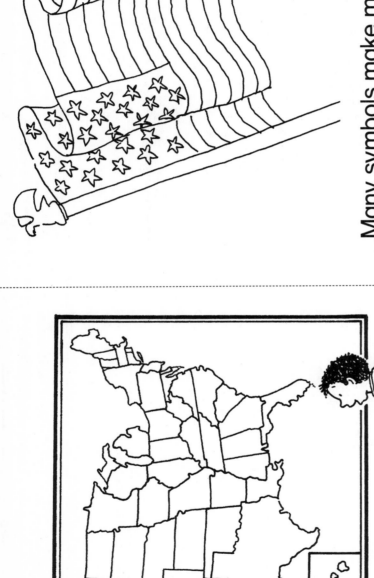

My country is the United States
of America.
For short I call it the U.S.A.!

1

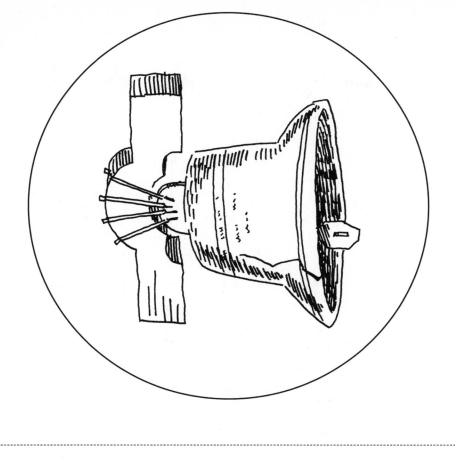

Another symbol is the

Liberty _____ .

It stands for our country's freedom.

4

Another symbol is the

bald _____ .

I see this symbol _____ .

3

Our Country Write & Read Books Scholastic Teaching Resources

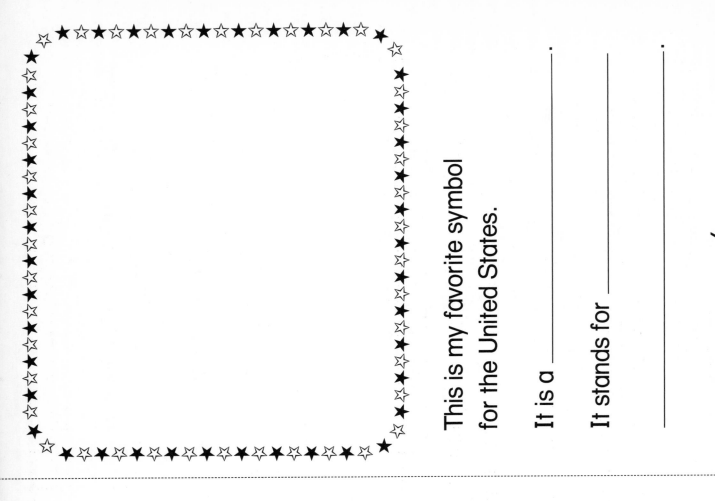

This is my favorite symbol for the United States.

It is a _____.

It stands for _____.

6

Another symbol is the

Statue of _____.

This symbol also stands for freedom.

5

Our Country Write & Read Books Scholastic Teaching Resources

We Honor Dr. King

by _____

What else do you know about Martin Luther King, Jr.? Draw a picture and write about it.

5

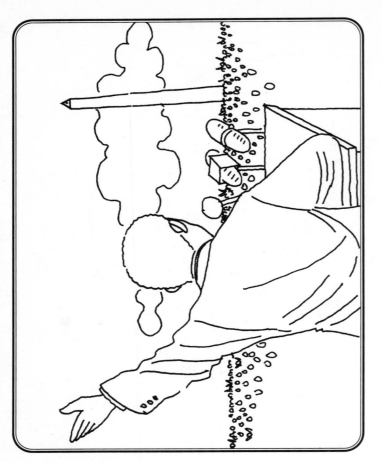

Dr. King was a speaker.

He spoke about _____

_____

_____

2

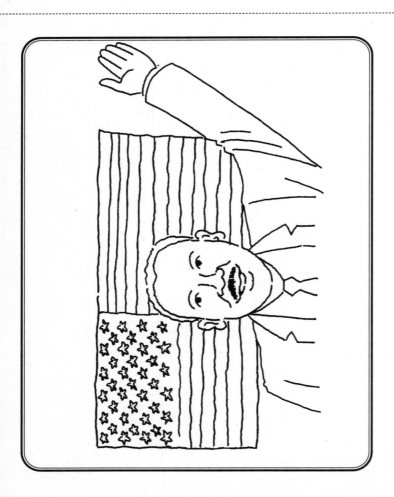

Dr. Martin Luther King, Jr., was a leader.

He led people to _____

_____

_____

1

Dr. King was a dreamer.

He dreamed that _____

_____

_____

4

Dr. King was a writer.

He wrote about _____

_____

3

Our Country Write & Read Books Scholastic Teaching Resources

I can follow Dr. King's dream for peace.

I can _____

_____ .

6

We honor Dr. King every January.

We remember that he _____

_____ .

5

I Celebrate Presidents' Day!

by _____

What else do you know about Presidents' Day? Draw a picture and write about it.

9

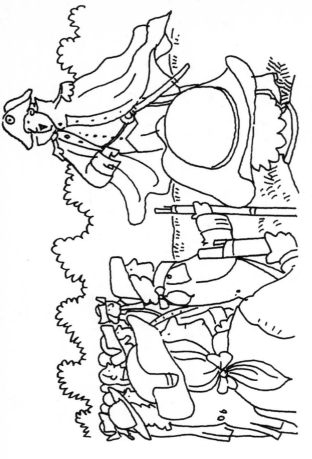

was our country's first president.

He led our country in a war
against England.

He helped the United States
become a new country.

2

On Presidents' Day, we honor our
past presidents.
Two of our great presidents

were _____

_____

and _____ .

1

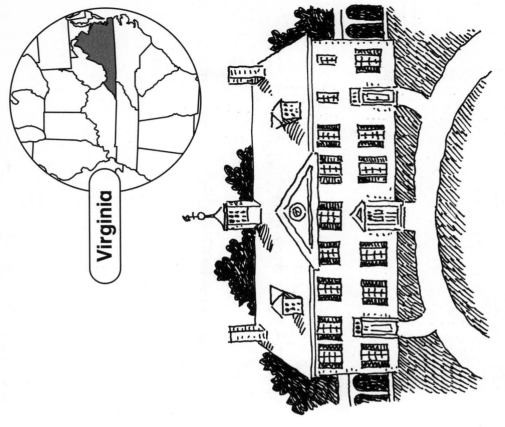

Virginia

On Presidents' Day, I can learn
about Mount Vernon.
It was Washington's home
in _____ .

4

_____
was the 16th president.
He led our country during
the Civil War.
He helped many Americans
become free.

3

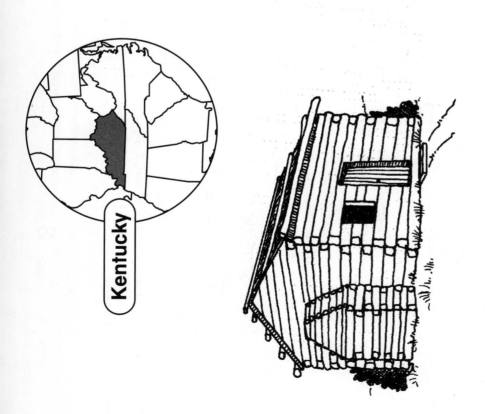

I can learn that Washington is called the "father of his country."
He got this name because _____
_____
_____.

6

Kentucky

I can learn about Lincoln's first home.
It was a log cabin in _____.

5

On Presidents' Day, I can wear
a three-cornered hat like

_____.

I can wear a stovepipe hat like

_____.

8

I can learn that Lincoln was called
"Honest Abe."
He got this name because _____

_____.

7

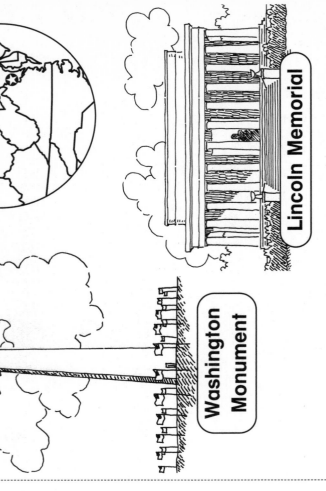

Washington, D.C.

Lincoln Memorial

Washington Monument

I can learn about places that honor

two great _____.

I can visit these monuments in _____.

10

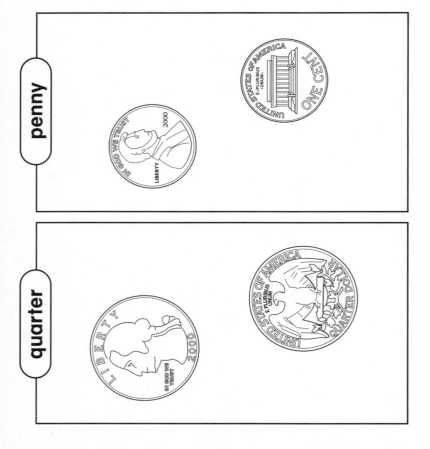

penny

quarter

I can look at pictures of Washington
and Lincoln on coins.

Washington is on a _____.

Lincoln is on a _____.

9

Happy Birthday, America!

by _____

What else do you know about Independence Day? Draw a picture and write about it.

_____

_____

_____

_____

5

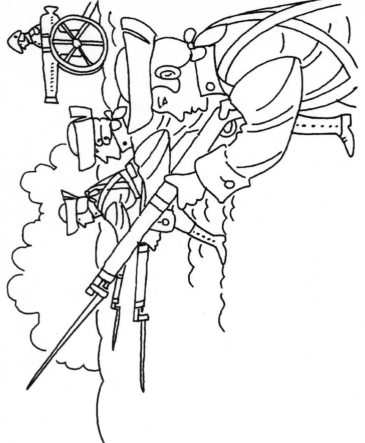

Many years ago, America was ruled
by England.
The two countries went to war.
On July 4, 1776, America declared

that it was _____ .

2

Our country has a birthday.
It is called Independence Day.

It is on July _____ .

1

On this day, we hang the
American flag.

4

Today Americans celebrate
Independence Day.
We celebrate because we are free.

3

On this day, we celebrate with parades.

We see _____.

We hear _____.

6

On this day, we wear the colors _____,

and _____.

5

On this day, I celebrate my country's birthday.

I _____

8

On this day, we celebrate with fireworks.

We see _____

We hear _____

7

We Are Voters

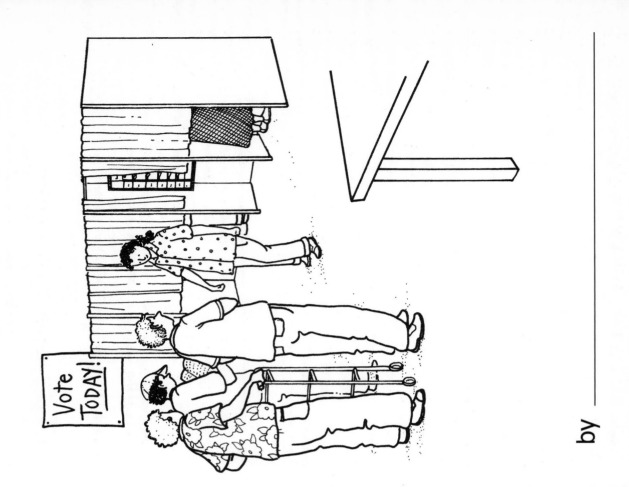

Vote TODAY!

by _____

What else do you know about voting?
Draw a picture and write about it.

_____

_____

_____

Sometimes students vote in school.

Students can vote about _____

2

We are voters when we vote!

A fair way to agree about choices is

to _____.

1

Another way to vote is to raise

our _____ .

We count the votes.

The choice with the most votes wins.

4

One way to vote is to _____

our choices on paper.

We count the votes.

The choice with the most votes wins.

3

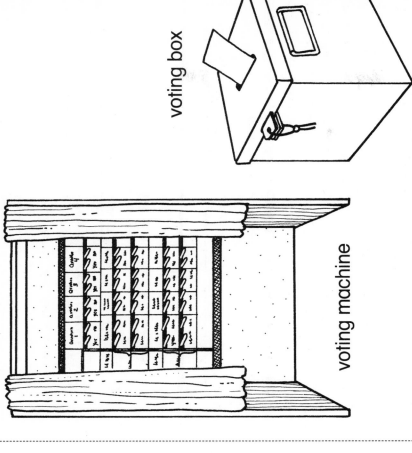

voting box

voting machine

On Election Day, many voters use a voting machine. Others use a voting box. I would like to use a _____.

6

Adults vote for leaders on Election Day. Election Day is on the first Tuesday in _____.

5

Our Country Write & Read Books Scholastic Teaching Resources

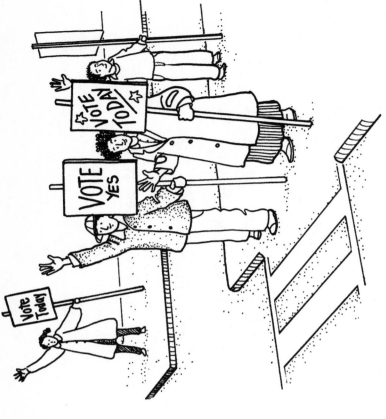

The people with the most _____ are elected.

They work in their new job for a certain amount of time. Someday voters will choose new leaders for these jobs.

8

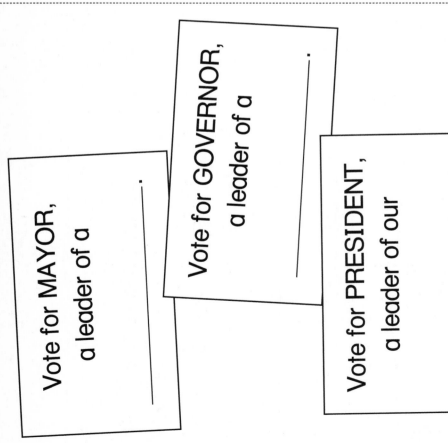

Vote for MAYOR, a leader of a _____ .

Vote for GOVERNOR, a leader of a _____ .

Vote for PRESIDENT, a leader of our _____ .

On Election Day, voters choose leaders of the government. These leaders help run communities, states, and the country.

7

We Give
Thanks

by _____

What else do you know about Thanksgiving? Draw a picture and write about it.

5

On this holiday, we remember

the _____

and the first Thanksgiving.

2

Americans celebrate

_____

on the fourth Thursday
in November.
It is a holiday for giving thanks.

1

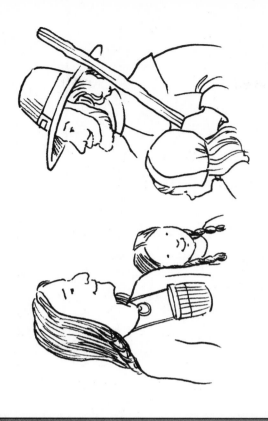

The Wampanoag were
Native Americans.
They lived in America long before
the _____ arrived.

4

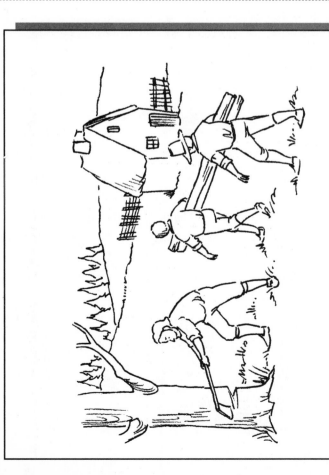

The Pilgrims' first year in America
was very hard.

They had little _____ to eat.
They had to build places to _____ .

3

By the end of the year, the Pilgrims had a good harvest.

They planned a _____
to celebrate.

6

The Wampanoag helped the Pilgrims.

They showed the Pilgrims how to use fish to grow _____.

5

On Thanksgiving, we give thanks for many things.

I give thanks for _____.

8

The Pilgrims and the Wampanoag shared a feast.

This was the first _____.

7

The First Americans

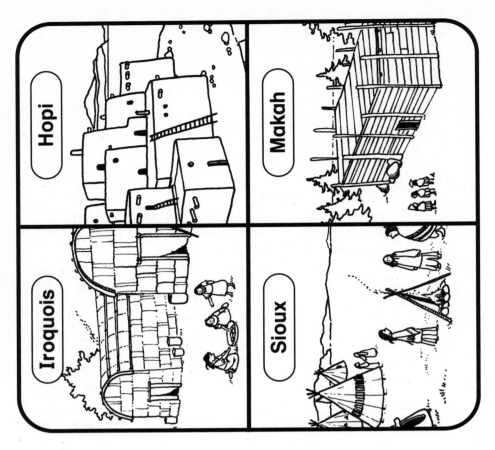

Hopi

Makah

Iroquois

Sioux

by _____

Our Country Write & Read Books Scholastic Teaching Resources

What else do you know about Native Americans? Draw a picture and write about it.

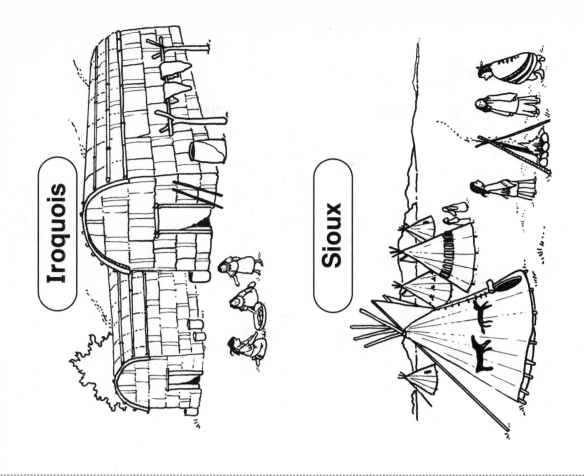

Iroquois

Sioux

Long ago, Native Americans lived in many different groups.

2

The first people in America were Native Americans. They have lived here for thousands of years.

1

Native Americans long ago used things from nature to meet their needs.

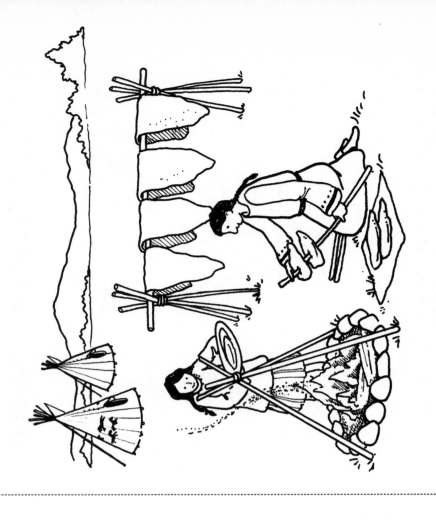

Animals gave them _____ _____ .

4

Hopi

Makah

Each group had a different _____ .

They still use these group names today.

3

Our Country Write & Read Books Scholastic Teaching Resources

Iroquois

The _____ lived

in longhouses in forests.

They hunted, fished, and farmed.

6

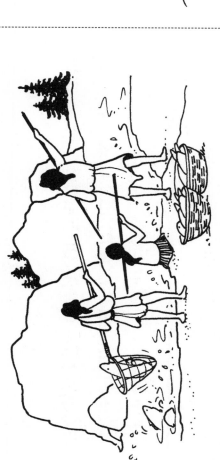

Bodies of water gave them _____

_____.

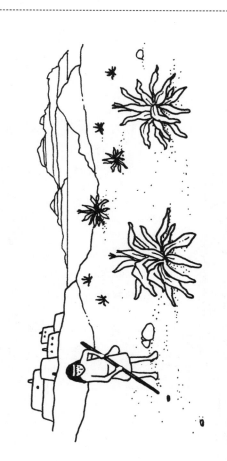

Plants and trees gave them _____

_____.

5

Sioux

The _____ hunted
buffalo on the plains.
They moved their tipi homes from
place to place.

8

Hopi

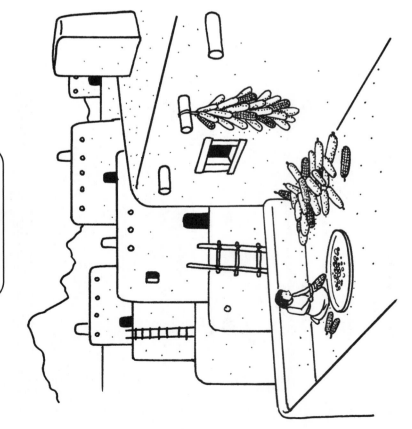

The _____ lived
in pueblos in the desert.
Their homes were made of clay.
They grew corn for food.

7

The _____ live
_____ in my state or region.
Long ago, their homes were _____.

They _____.

10

Makah

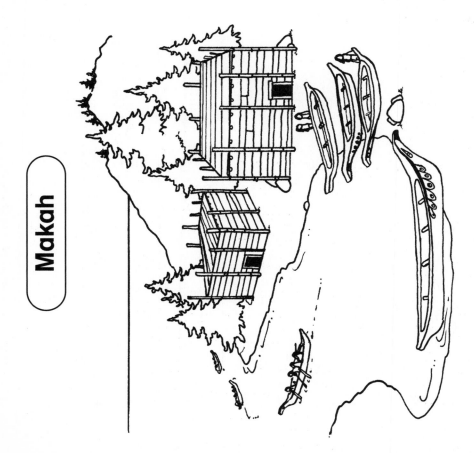

The _____ lived
near forests by the Pacific Ocean.
They built wooden homes.
They hunted whales and fished.

9

Thank You, Inventors!

by _____

What else do you know about inventors?
Draw a picture and write about it.

Alexander Graham Bell

I can call a friend from home.
Thanks to Mr. Bell, I use the

_____.

2

Let's give a cheer for inventors!
Hip, hip, hooray!
They get ideas for new things

that I use every _____.

1

Our Country Write & Read Books Scholastic Teaching Resources

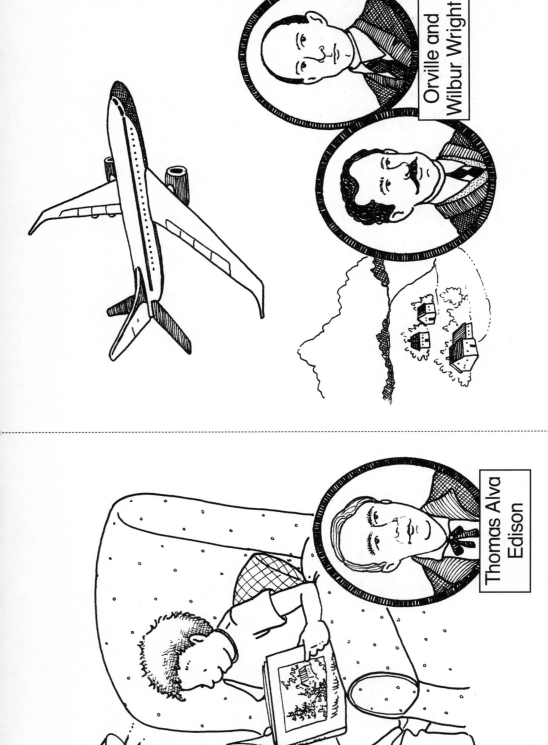

Airplanes carry me up in the sky.
Thanks to the Wright brothers,

Orville and Wilbur Wright

airplanes _____ .

4

When it is dark, I turn on a light.
Thanks to Mr. Edison, lightbulbs

Thomas Alva Edison

make rooms _____ .

3

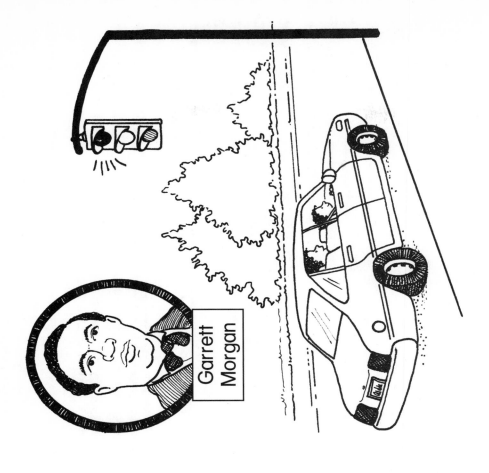

Garrett Morgan

We see its red, yellow, and green
spots glow.
Thanks to Mr. Morgan's traffic light,

we stop, slow down, and _____!

6

Edwin Binney
and Harold Smith

I use crayons in colors
like red, green, and blue.
Thanks to Mr. Binney and Mr. Smith,
I draw pictures and

_____ them, too!

5

If I could invent something, I would

invent _____ .

8

A paper bag can hold a bunch.
Thanks to Ms. Knight, one carries

my _____ .

7

My Great State

State's Name _____

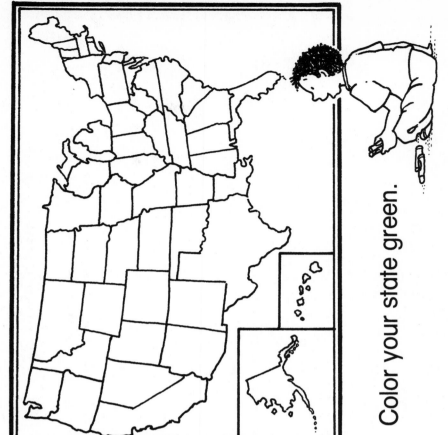

Color your state green.

by _____

Our Country Write & Read Books Scholastic Teaching Resources

What else do you know about your state? Draw a picture and write about it.

_____

_____

_____

_____

_____

1

My state has places to visit.
One place I like to visit is

_____

_____

2

Greetings From

_____!

My state is part of the
United States of America.

Its name is

_____

1

My state has a capital city.
Leaders of my state work there.
The capital's name is

_____.

4

Something I like to do in this place is

_____.

3

My state's flower is _____

My state's tree is _____

6

My state has symbols.
One symbol is the flag.
This is what my state's flag looks like:

_____

_____

5

Our Country Write & Read Books Scholastic Teaching Resources

My state has a nickname.
Its nickname is _____.

8

My state's bird is _____.

My state's animal is _____.

7

I like living in my state because

_____

_____.

10

My state has a history.
One thing that happened in my state

was _____

_____.

9

My Travel Book

by _____

What else do you know about these or other places? Draw a picture and write about it.

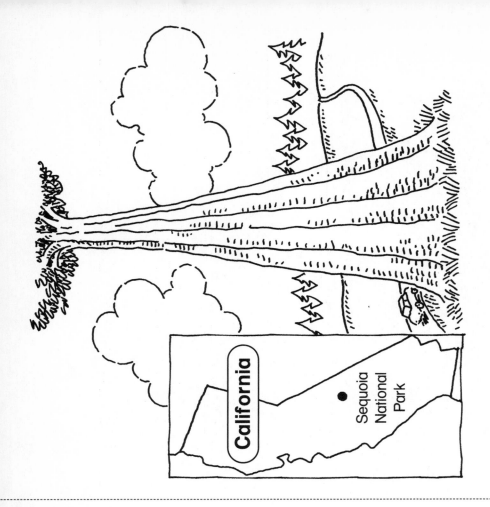

I can visit Sequoia National Park in

_____ .

Some of the trees there are more than 200 feet tall!

2

Our country has many things to see and places to visit.

1

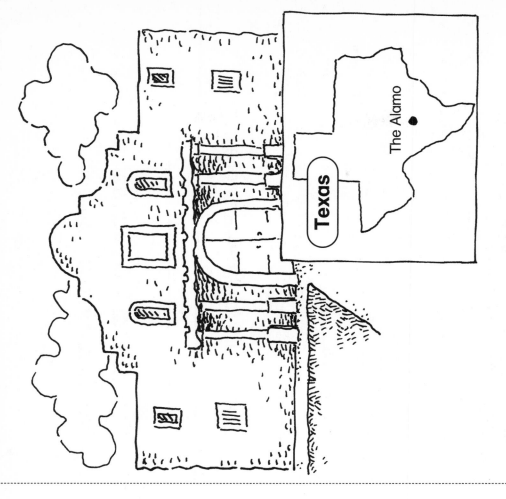

I can visit the Alamo in

_____.

A battle once took place at this fort.

4

I can visit Cliff Palace in

_____.

Long ago, Native Americans
built this city under a cliff.

3

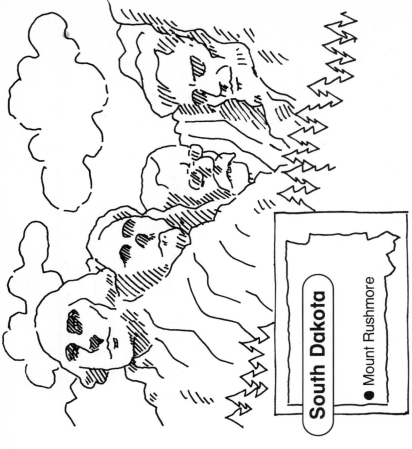

I can visit Mount Rushmore in
_____ .

The faces of four presidents
are carved into a mountain.

6

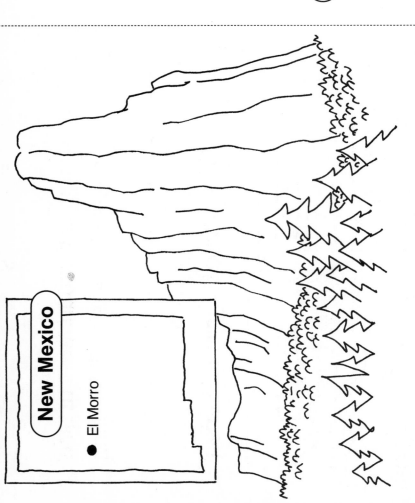

I can visit El Morro in
_____ .

Native Americans and settlers
carved pictures and names
in the rock.

5

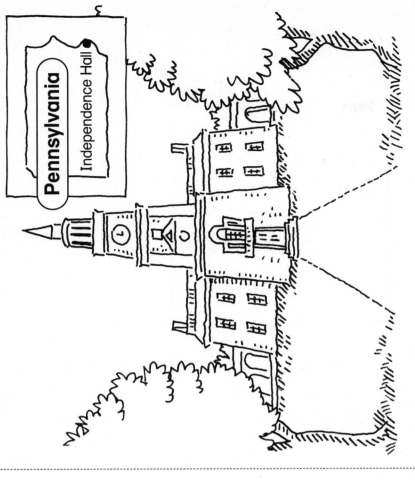

I can visit Independence Hall in

_____.

This is where the Declaration
of Independence was signed.

8

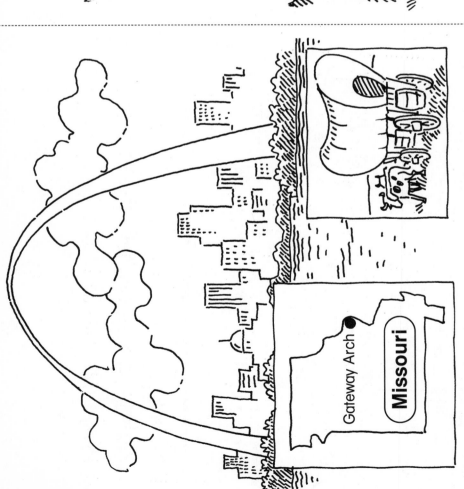

I can visit the Gateway Arch in

_____.

This monument was built
to honor the pioneers.

7

I can also visit _____

in _____

This is _____

10

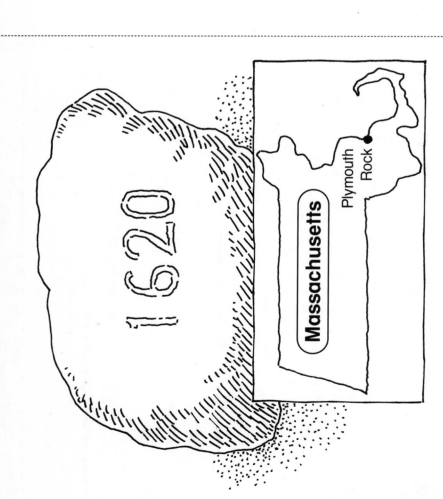

I can visit Plymouth Rock in _____

Some say this is where the Pilgrims came to shore in 1620.

9

Our Country Write & Read Books Scholastic Teaching Resources

Washington, D.C., Our Capital

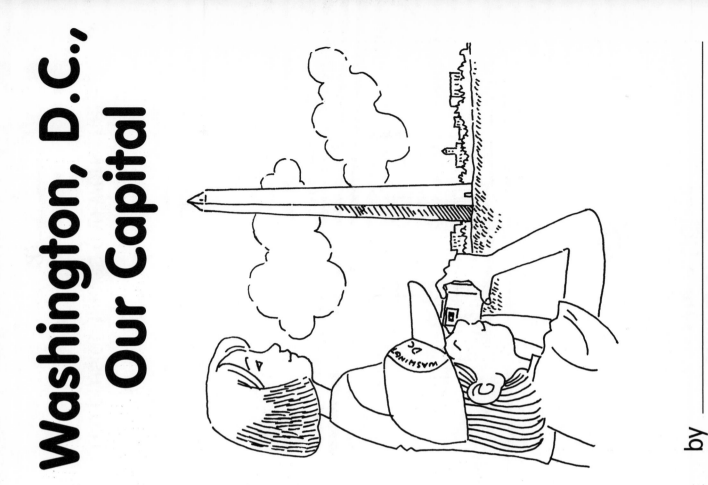

by _____

What else do you know about Washington, D.C.? Draw a picture and write about it.

3

White House

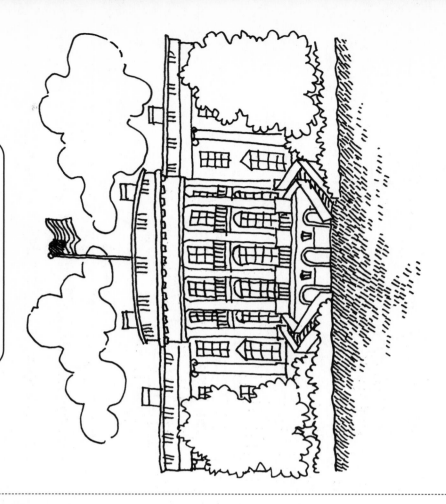

Our capital has important buildings.

This is the _____ .
The president lives and works here.

2

United States of America

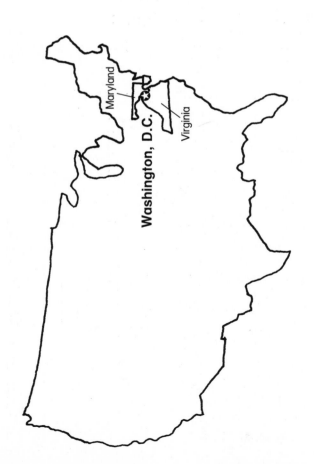

Maryland

Washington, D.C.

Virginia

Washington, D.C., is an important city.
It is the capital of the United States.

1

Our Country Write & Read Books Scholastic Teaching Resources

Washington Monument

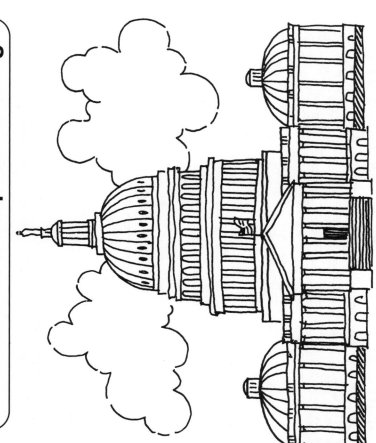

Our capital has monuments.

This is the _____

This monument honors our first president, George Washington.

4

United States Capitol Building

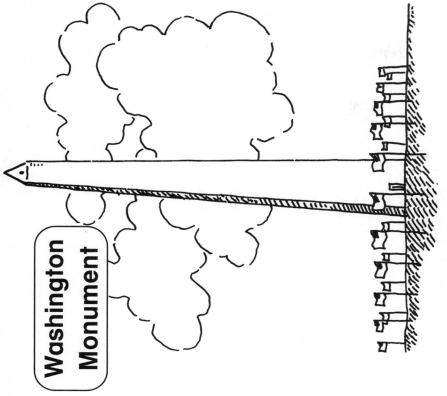

This is the _____

Our country's laws, or rules, are made here.

3

Vietnam Veterans Memorial

Our capital has memorials to honor our soldiers.
A memorial helps us remember people or events.

This is the _____.

6

Lincoln Memorial

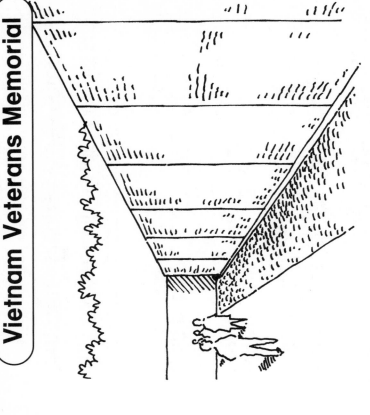

This is the _____.

This monument honors our 16th

president, _____.

5

National Air and Space Museum

Our capital has museums.

This is the National _____
_____ Museum.

It shows things used for air and

space travel, such as _____
_____.

8

World War II Memorial

This is the _____
_____.

It helps us remember _____
_____.

7

This is _____
It _____

10

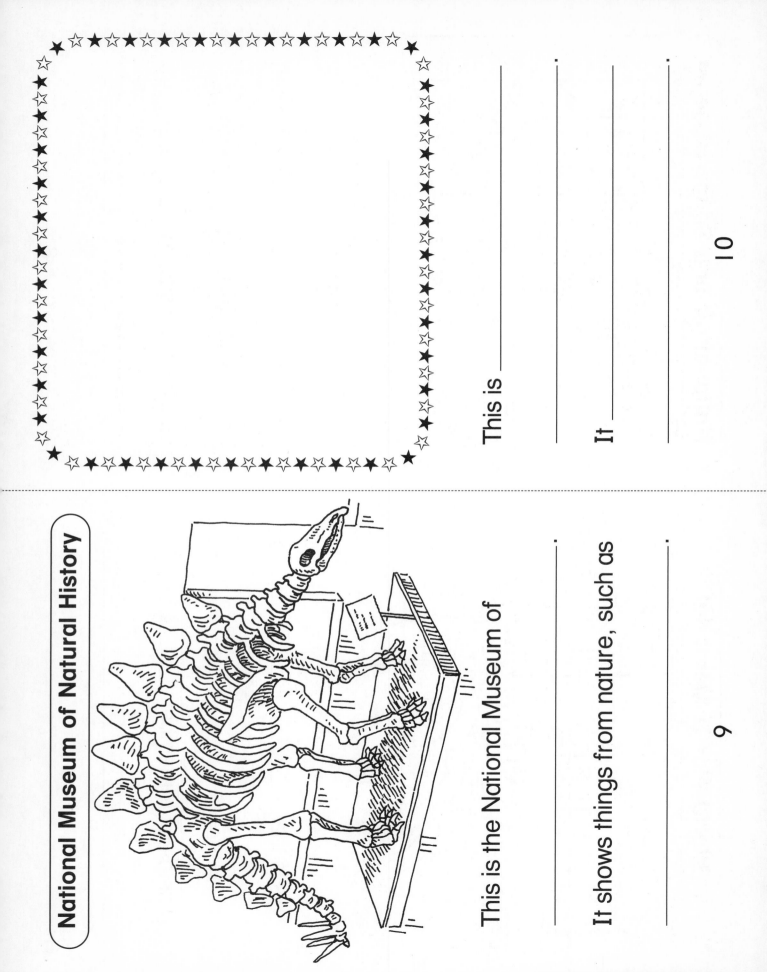

National Museum of Natural History

This is the National Museum of _____

It shows things from nature, such as _____

9

United States Geography Riddles

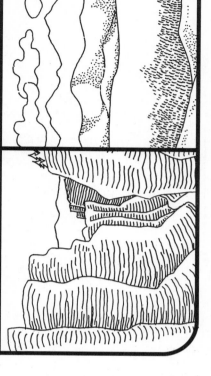

by _____

What else do you know about United States geography? Draw a picture and write about it.

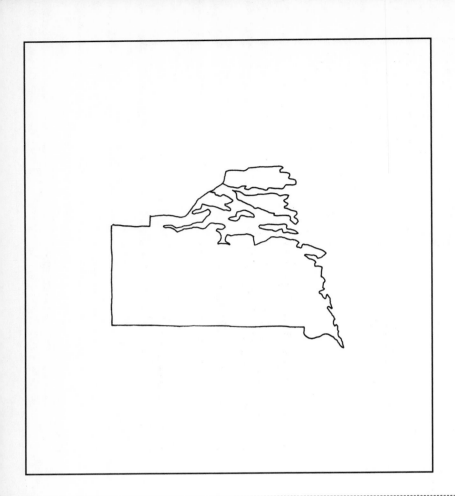

I am the smallest state.
I am in the northeast.

My name is _____.

2

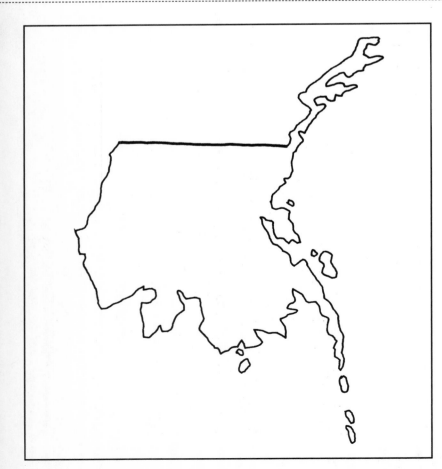

I am the biggest state
in the United States.
I am in the northwest.

My name is _____.

1

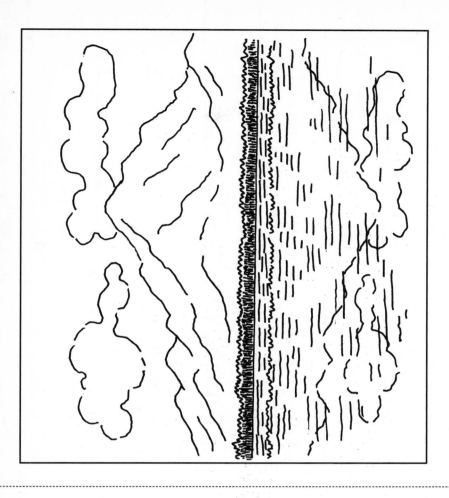

I am the tallest mountain
in the United States.
I am in the Alaska Range.

My name is _____
_____.

4

I am the only island state.
I am in the Pacific Ocean.

My name is _____
_____.

3

Our Country Write & Read Books Scholastic Teaching Resources

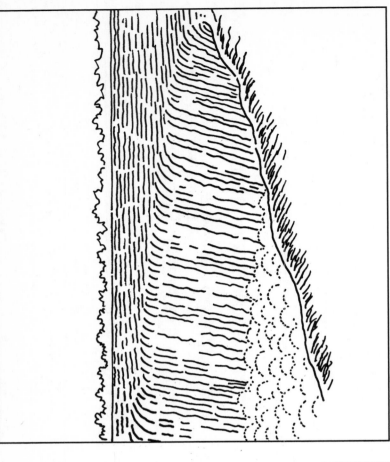

I am a large waterfall.
I am in New York and Canada.

My name is _____ .

6

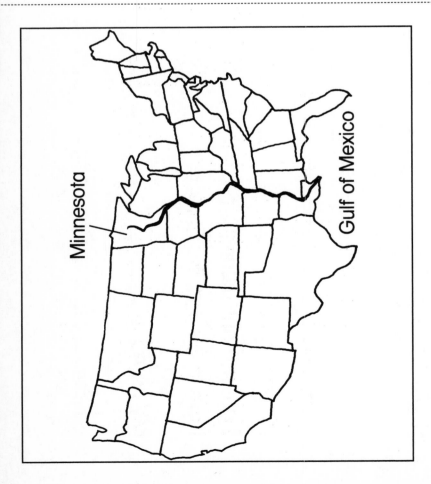

Minnesota

Gulf of Mexico

I am a long river.
I flow from Minnesota
to the Gulf of Mexico.

My name is _____ .

5

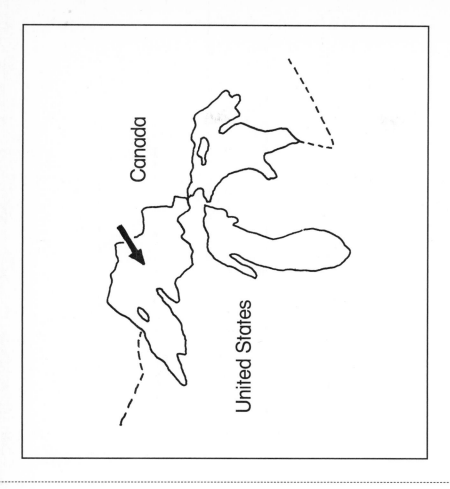

I am the hottest and driest place in the United States.
I am a desert in California and Nevada.

My name is _____

7

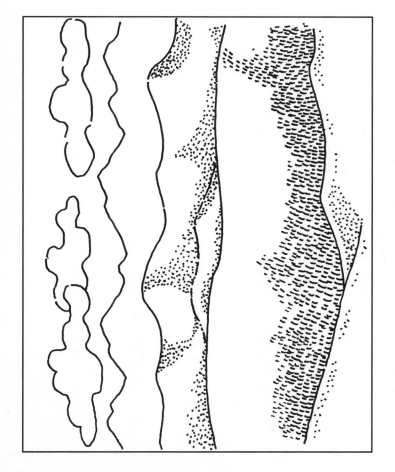

Canada

United States

I am the largest freshwater lake.
I am between Canada and the United States.

My name is _____

8

Our Country Write & Read Books Scholastic Teaching Resources

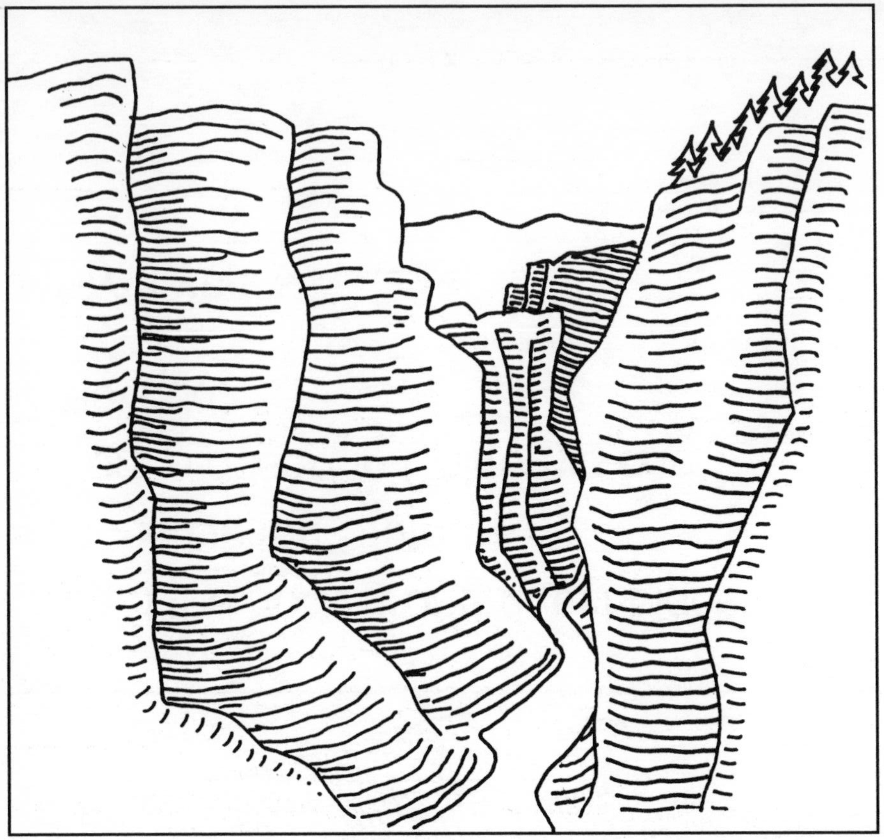

Write your own riddle!

I am _____.

I am _____.

My name is _____.

10

I am a deep valley formed by a river.
I am in Arizona.

My name is _____.

9

Our Government

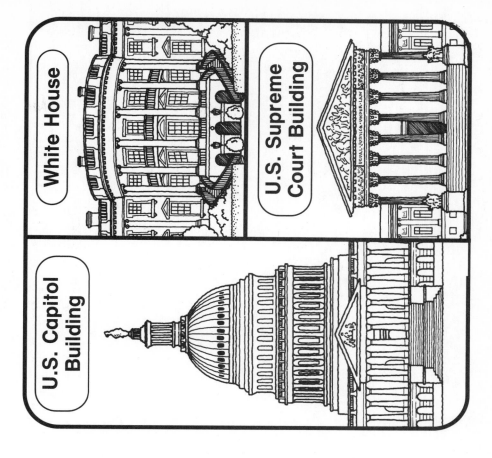

U.S. Capitol Building

White House

U.S. Supreme Court Building

by _____

What else do you know about our country's government? Draw a picture and write about it.

5

Our country has laws.
Laws are rules we must follow.

One law I follow is _____

_____ .

2

Americans vote for leaders.

These _____ run our
communities, states, and country.
They form our government.

1

Our Country Write & Read Books Scholastic Teaching Resources

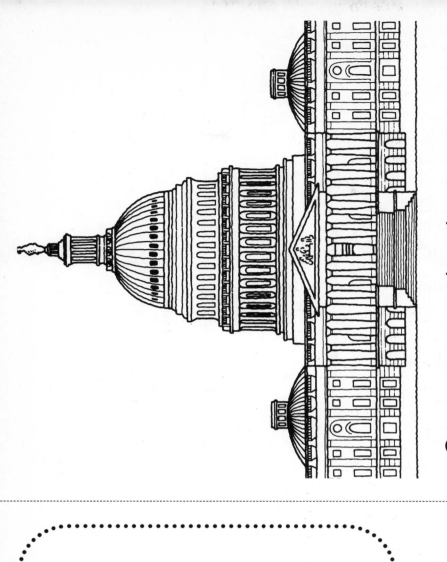

Our government has three parts.
Congress is one part.
This group of leaders makes laws for

our _____ .
They work in the Capitol Building
in Washington, D.C.

4

Our country has laws that give
people rights.
A right is something we can have
or do.

We have the right to _____ .

3

The Supreme Court is the third part of our government.

The _____ Court has nine judges.
They make sure our laws are fair.
They work in the Supreme Court Building.

6

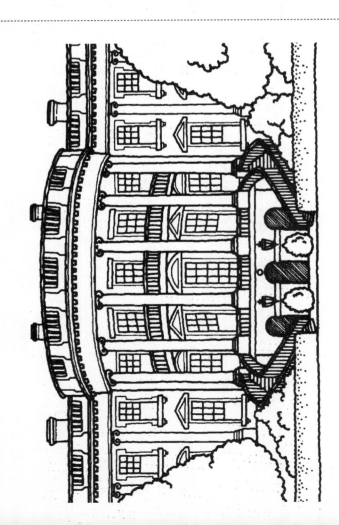

The president is the second part.
This leader runs our country.
The president lives and works in the _____.

5

Welcome to the White House!

by _____

Our Country Write & Read Books Scholastic Teaching Resources

What else do you know about the White House? Draw a picture and write about it.

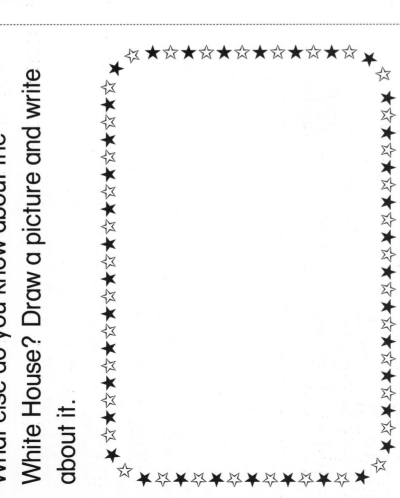

_____

_____

_____

_____

89

The _____ lives and
works in the White House.
The president is the leader of the
United States.

2

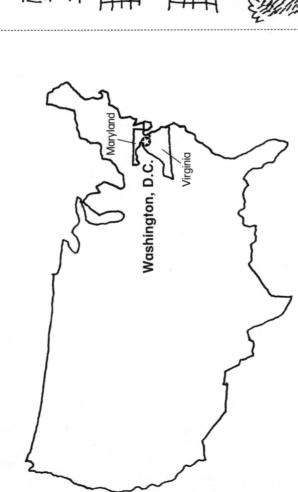

The White House is in

_____ .

It is in our nation's capital.

1

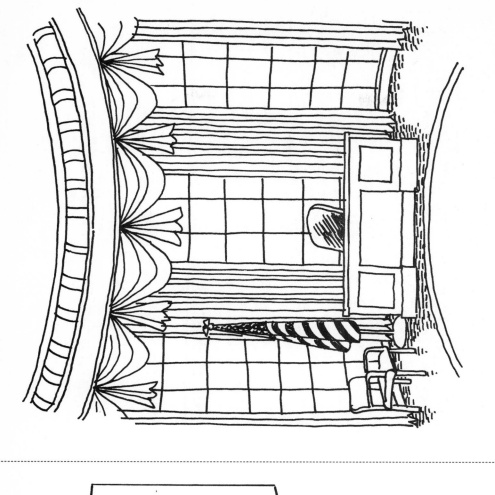

The Oval Office is the room where

the president works.

It is called this because it is shaped

like an _____ .

4

Every four years, people _____

to decide who will be the president.

3

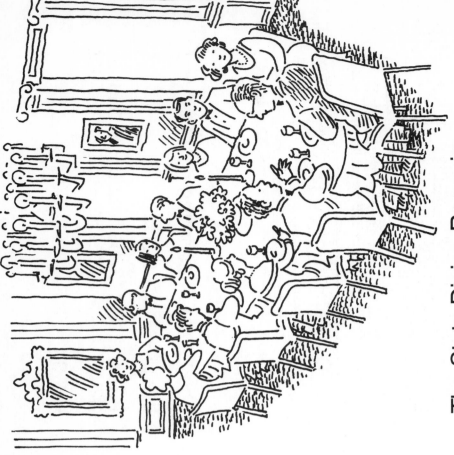

The State Dining Room is for special dinners.

The president's guests _____ in this room.

6

The Brady Press Briefing Room is where people learn news about our country.

Reporters ask _____.

Then they share the information with the country and world.

5

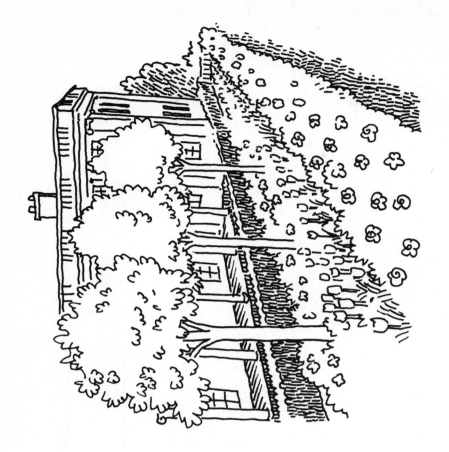

The White House has beautiful
_____.

Many kinds of flowers, bushes, and trees grow in the gardens.

8

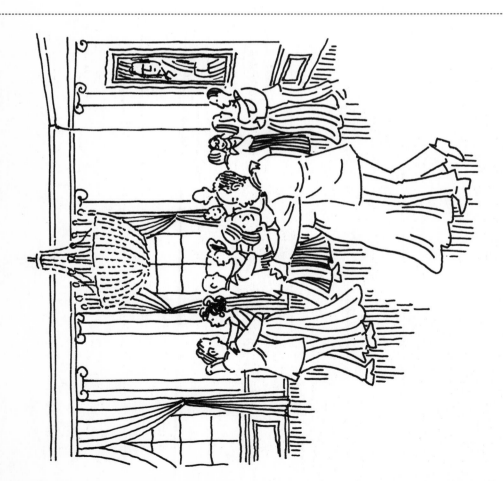

The East Room is a large room for special events.
Sometimes the president's guests _____ in this room.

7

3

This is a picture of the author,
_____.

About the Author

The author of this book is _____
_____.

is _____ years old
and lives in _____.

The author likes to _____,
_____, and
_____.

5

Notes